STICKER YOUR BRICKS

Style Your Building Brick Masterpieces with Reusable Stickers

STICKER YOUR BRICKS

Style Your Building Brick Masterpieces with Reusable Stickers

Amanda Brack

Sky Pony Press
New York

Sky Pony Press books may be purchased in bulk at special discounts for sales promotion, corporate gifts, fund-raising, or educational purposes. Special editions can also be created to specifications. For details, contact the Special Sales Department, Sky Pony Press, 307 West 36th Street, 11th Floor, New York, NY 10018 or info@skyhorsepublishing.com.

Sky Pony® is a registered trademark of Skyhorse Publishing, Inc.®, a Delaware corporation.

Visit our website at www.skyponypress.com.

10 9 8 7 6 5 4 3 2

Library of Congress Cataloging-in-Publication Data is available on file.

Manufactured in China, October 2016
This product conforms to CPSIA 2008

Library of Congress Cataloging-in-Publication Data is available on file.

Cover design by Brian Peterson
Cover photo credit Hollan Publishing, Inc.

Print ISBN: 978-1-5107-0722-1

Interior design by Joshua Barnaby

STICKER YOUR BRICKS

Style Your Building Brick Masterpieces with Reusable Stickers

INTRODUCTION

Welcome to *Sticker Your Bricks*, where all of your brick creations are made unique with incredible stickers! Look through each of these fun ideas for using stickers to make your brick towns, houses, and construction sites even better!

Add forests to the backgrounds of your brick towns, race cars down Route 66, and invite friendly robots onto your futuristic space stations! The possibilities are endless with *Sticker Your Bricks*! There are a variety of stickers for every occasion, so you never have to pick just one. From farm animals and helicopters to rocket ships and traffic signs, these stickers will add all sorts of creativity to your favorite toy!

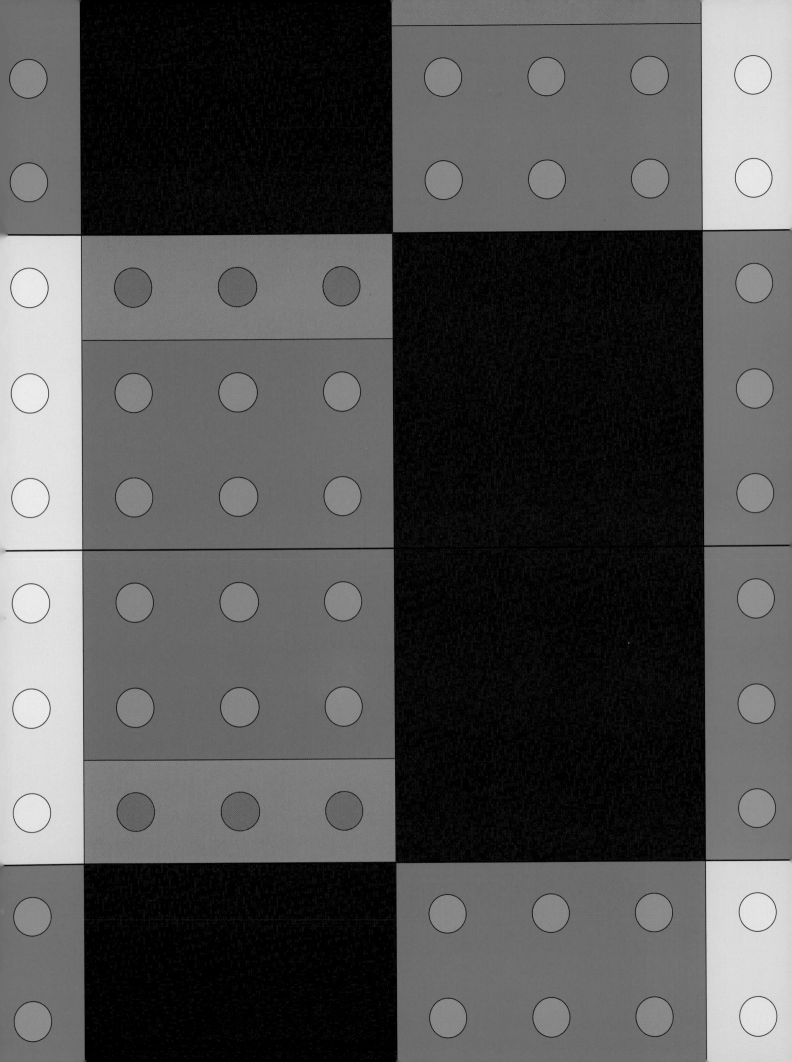

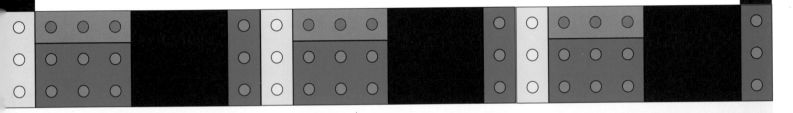

ICE CREAM TRUCK

Do you hear that music? It's the ice cream truck! Making a brick ice cream truck is a lot of fun, but what good is a frosty dessert truck without some awesome stickers? Add these frozen treat stickers to your truck so that the children know just what to buy while they're waiting in line.

FOOD TRUCK

Without a mix of some delicious-looking food stickers, this food truck is nothing but a hunk of metal on wheels. Have your brick people lining up in droves for the best-tasting food in town!

AUTO SHOP

Rev your engines! The old-timey garage posters and front ends of fancy cars are perfect for any mechanic's shop. Whether you set up your own auto body shop or race your cars on a speedway, these racecar stickers are the perfect accessory to your car creations!

SPACE

Alien invaders! Launch your way to the future with these cool robot and rocket ship stickers. Make your own spaceship or space station for when you want to travel across the universe. Have futuristic robots help you on your way!

SPACE SHIPS

These stickers are out of this world! There are so many options to choose from with these space ships—you can use them to decorate the walls of your brick creations, to build your own rocket launch pad, or to fly in a fleet of hovering alien space ships!

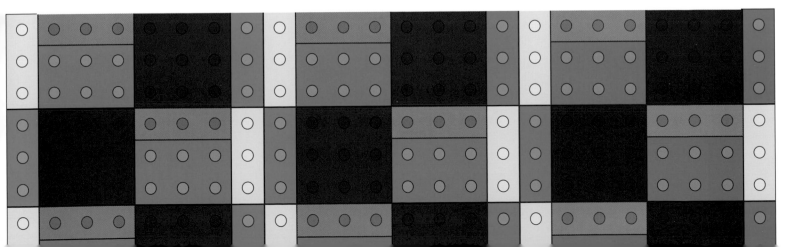

GAS STATION

Fill 'er up on Route 66! Sometimes called "The Main Street of America" or "The Mother Road," Route 66 is where great American road trips happen. Whether you're building a high-traffic speedway or a one-stop gas station for your brick towns, these stickers are just the way to go from zero to sixty!

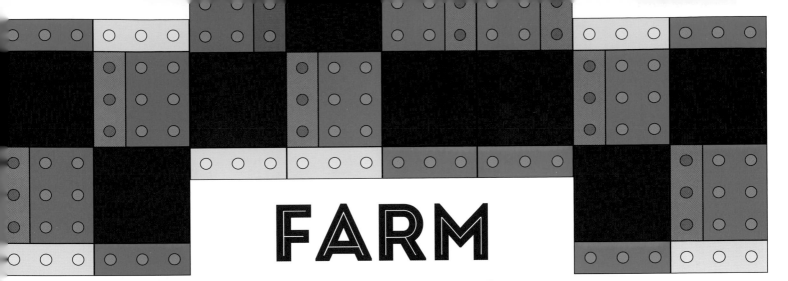

FARM

Time to work on the farm! Add some new animal friends to your barnyard using these adorable stick-on creatures. From kittens slinking across the barn doors to sheep grazing in the yard, there are endless ways to make your brick farm look just like the real thing.

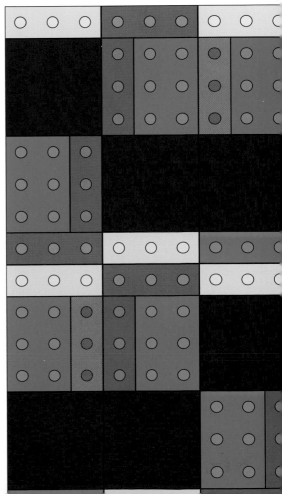

FIRE TRUCK

Here to save the day! Make sure your fire engines have the fire hoses they need! The fire department stickers go great on fire trucks, but they can also decorate any number of brick buildings.

CONSTRUCTION

Hard hat area! When you're building on a construction site, you need all sorts of big trucks and diggers to help you along. The crane helps bring heavy things to high places, the bulldozer moves things out of the way, and the digger lets construction workers dig deep into the ground for better buildings. These stickers are just like the real thing!

FLEET OF SHIPS

You sunk my battleship! When building your own fleet of ships on the sea, add some extra force with these cool ship stickers. Just pile up a few blue bricks over the water and this vessel will blend right in.

DINER

Order up! You can't have a retro diner without some cool signs. Decorate your brick restaurant with some of these great stickers, or add them to any wall you build to make them more fun!

ROAD SIGNS

Traffic jam! These great road signs can be decorative, or they can help direct the people in your brick towns to where they should go.

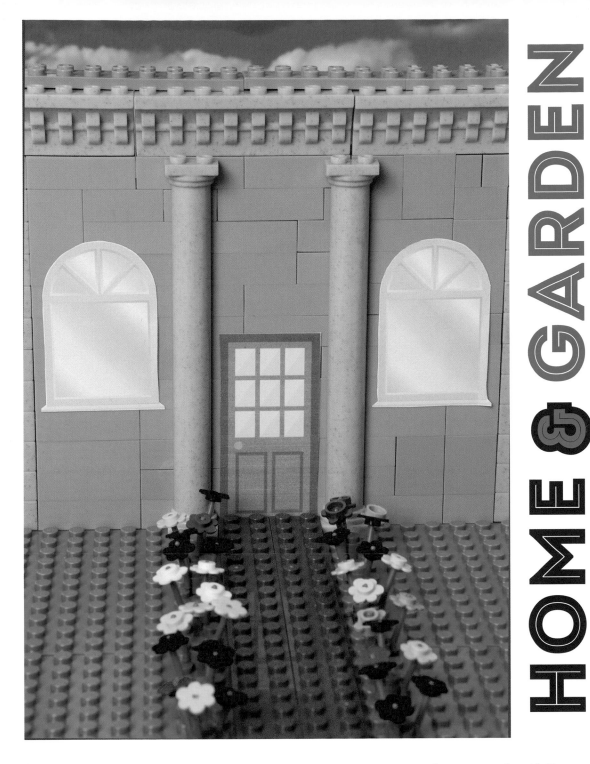

HOME & GARDEN

When one door closes, another one opens! Sticker your buildings with these big windows and doors to make your brick creations look just like real life homes, office buildings, or corner stores!

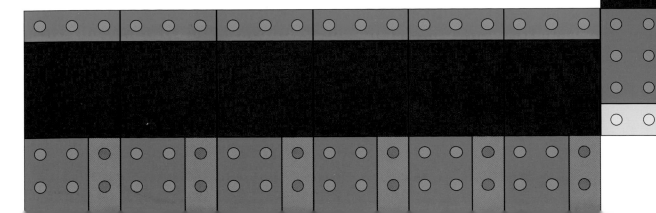

HOUSE

Sometimes brick houses can be a little dull all by themselves. Why not add some fun? Add a sticker garden or have your favorite pup playing in the yard. Mix and match your stickers for a super cool house that stands out!

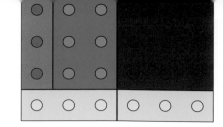

PICNIC

Let's go on a picnic! Use your tree stickers to create an outdoor scene: a forest, a pretty garden, or a nature trail. Your brick people will love roaming through thick woodsy areas, hiking in a rainforest, or just sitting outside and relaxing.

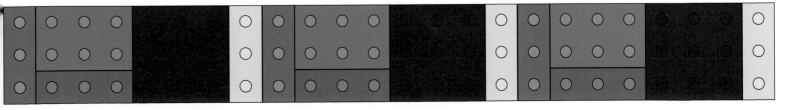

WARNING SIGNS

You're in the danger zone! Sticker your mad science lab, factory, construction site, or haunted building with these cool warning stickers. Ward off intruders, create windows for your submarine, or add detail to an iron building—just watch out for hazardous materials!

POLICE STATION

Make your game of "Cops and Robbers" even more life-like with these State Police stickers! Build your own police station, haul the bad guys off to jail, or put the police cruisers on patrol in your brick town!

BARBERSHOP
BEAUTY SALON

Snip, snip, snip! Build your own barbershop or beauty salon with these stylish stickers. The swirly barbershop pole and beauty parlor poster are just the right details for when your brick people are walking in to get a new 'do!

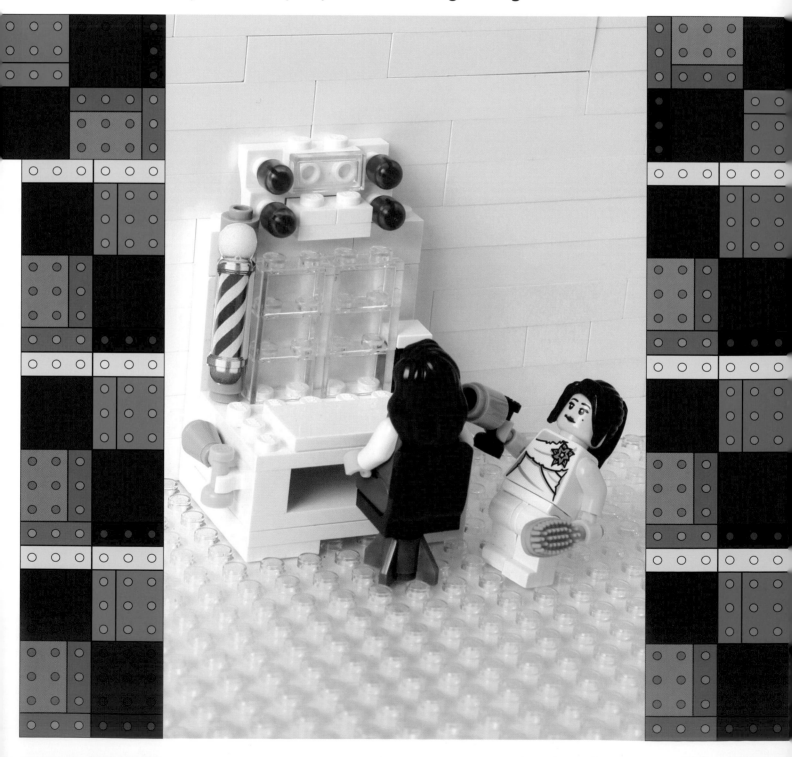

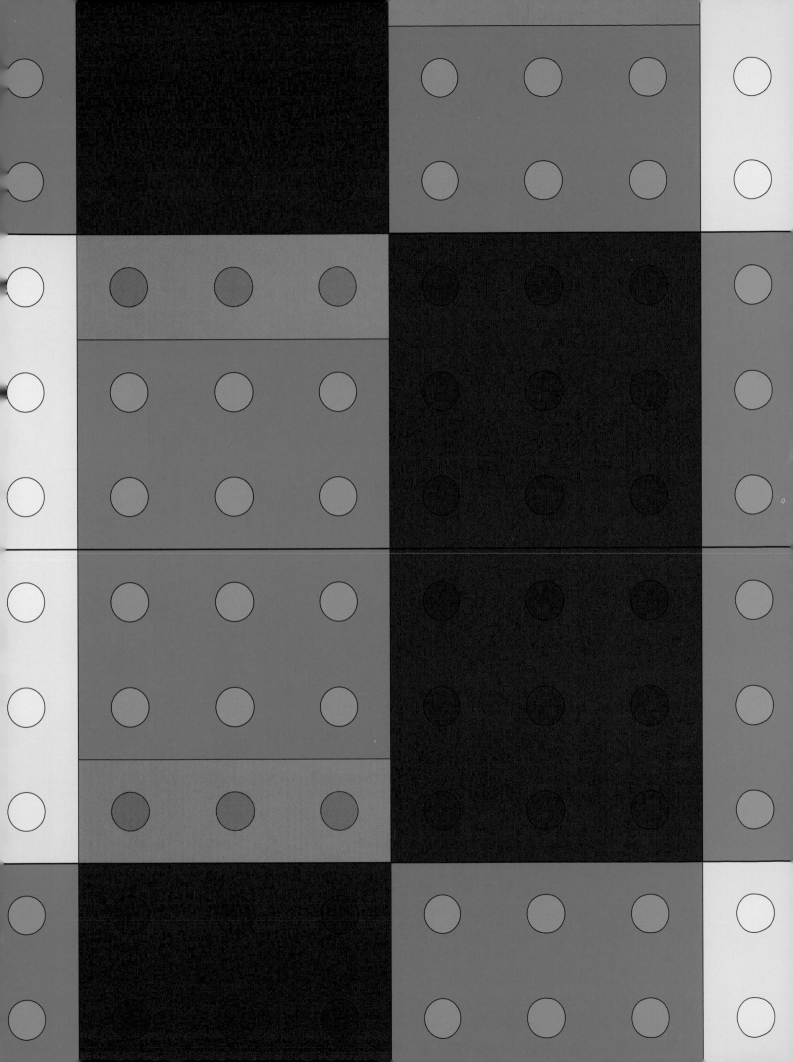

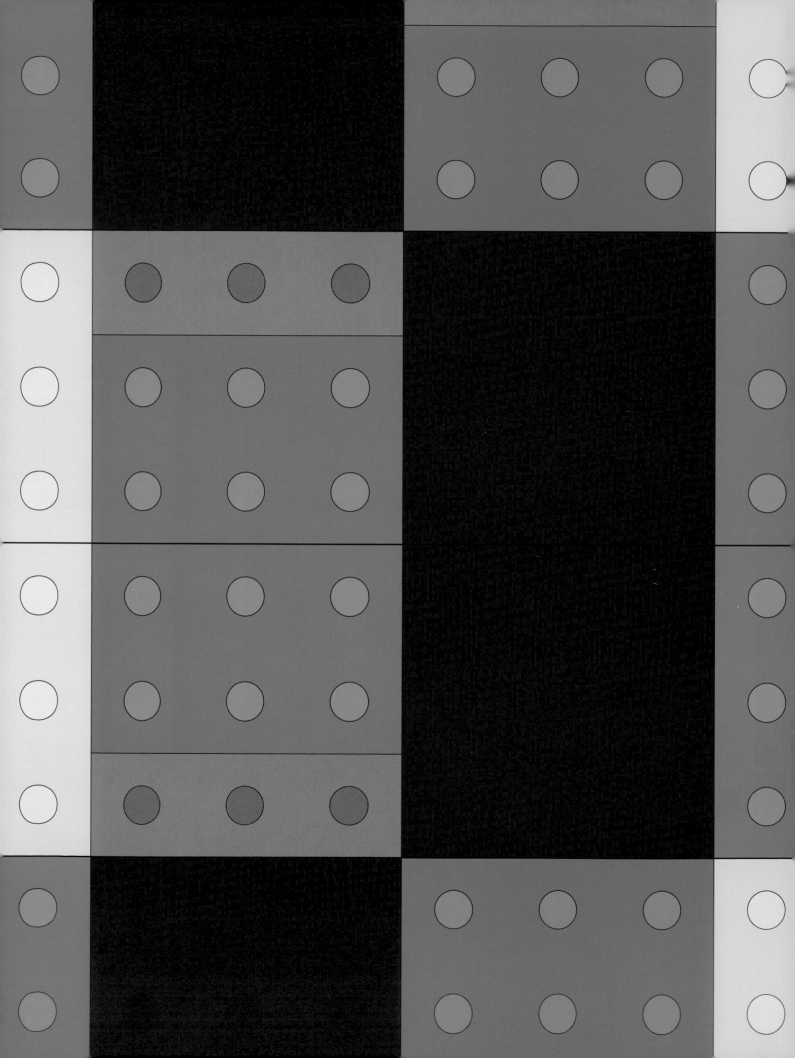

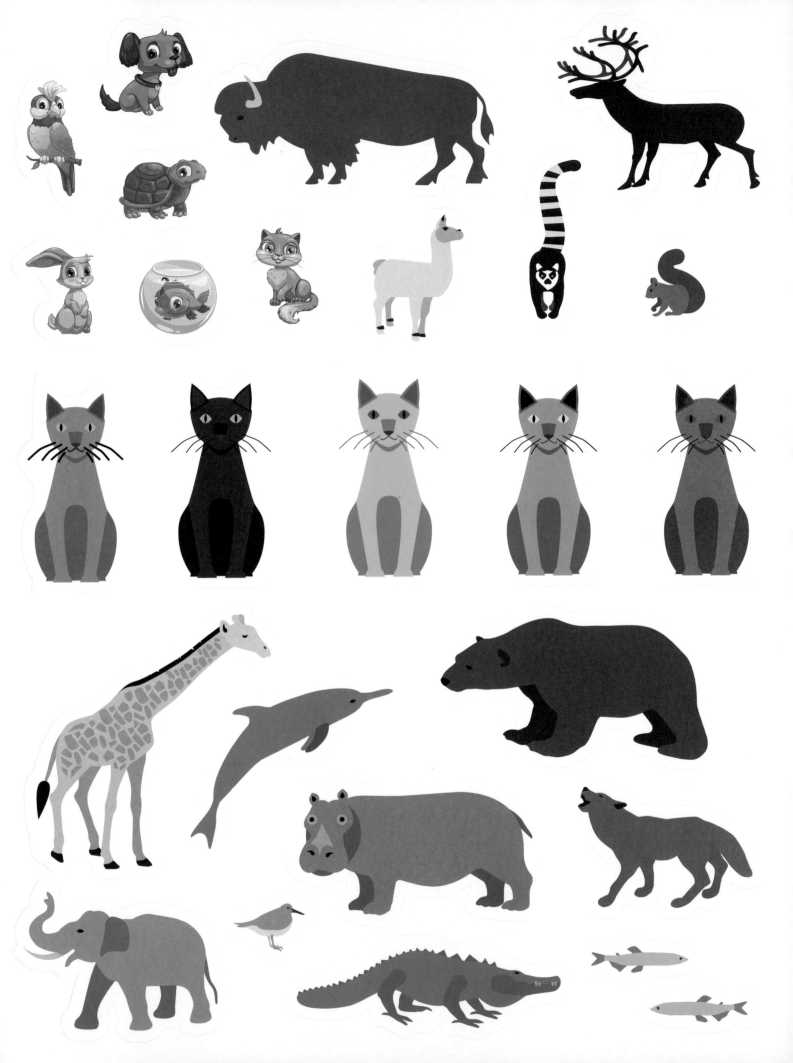

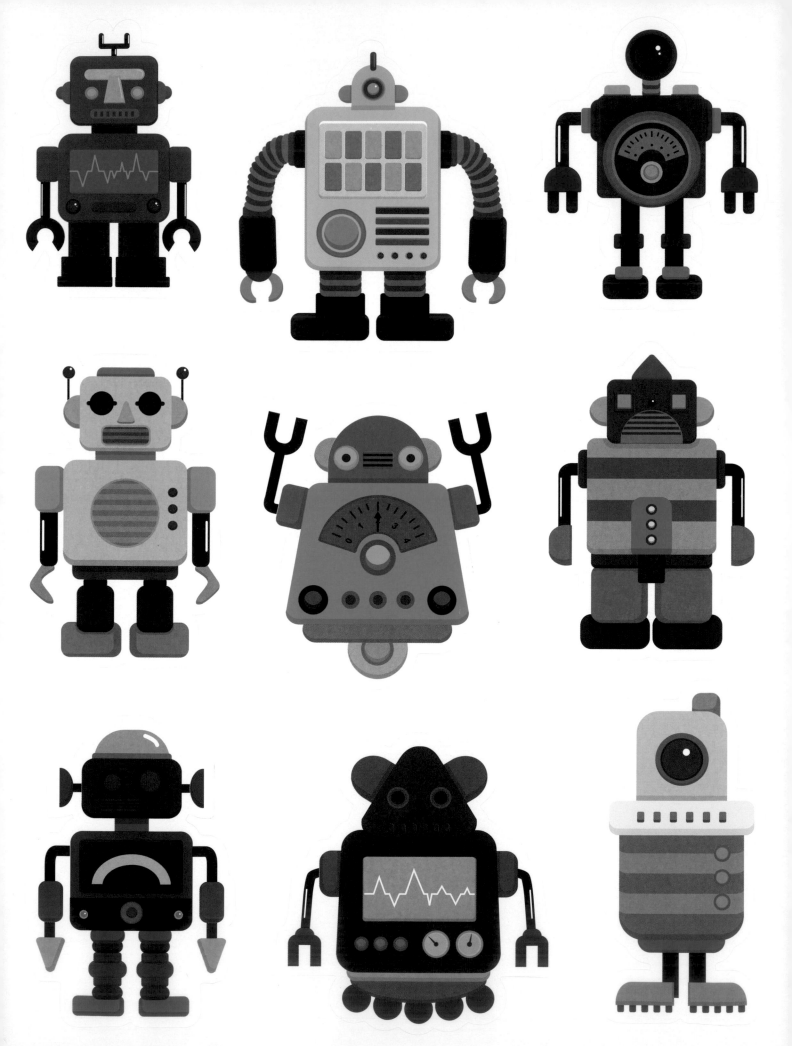

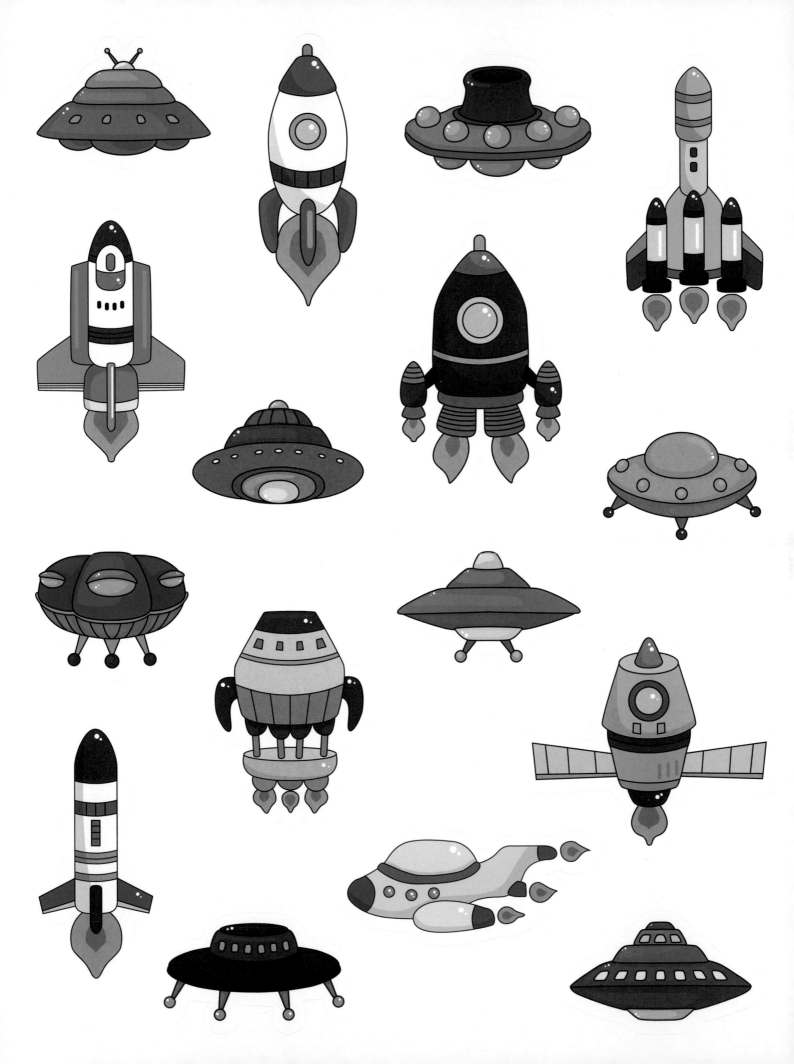

Hamburger

PIZZA

STOP

Burgers

ROUTE 66

Diner

Super Big Size

Burgers

COMPANY NAME

GARAGE

Mechanic On Duty

24 7

FULL SERVICE

Since 1960

TYRES · PETROLS · OILS

Route 66

GAS

OPEN 24 HOURS

RAIL CROSSING ROAD

Ice Cream

Ice Cream

ONE WAY

ONE WAY

Ice Cream

Ice Cream

DETOUR

ONE WAY

DO NOT

ENTER

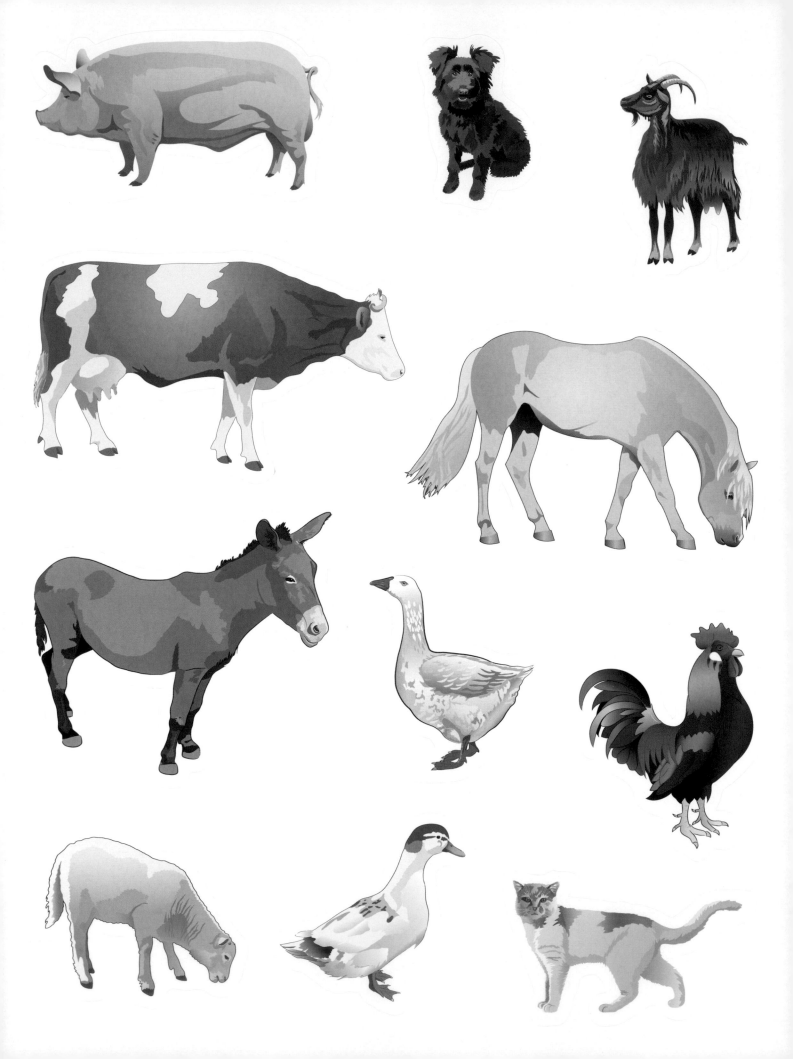

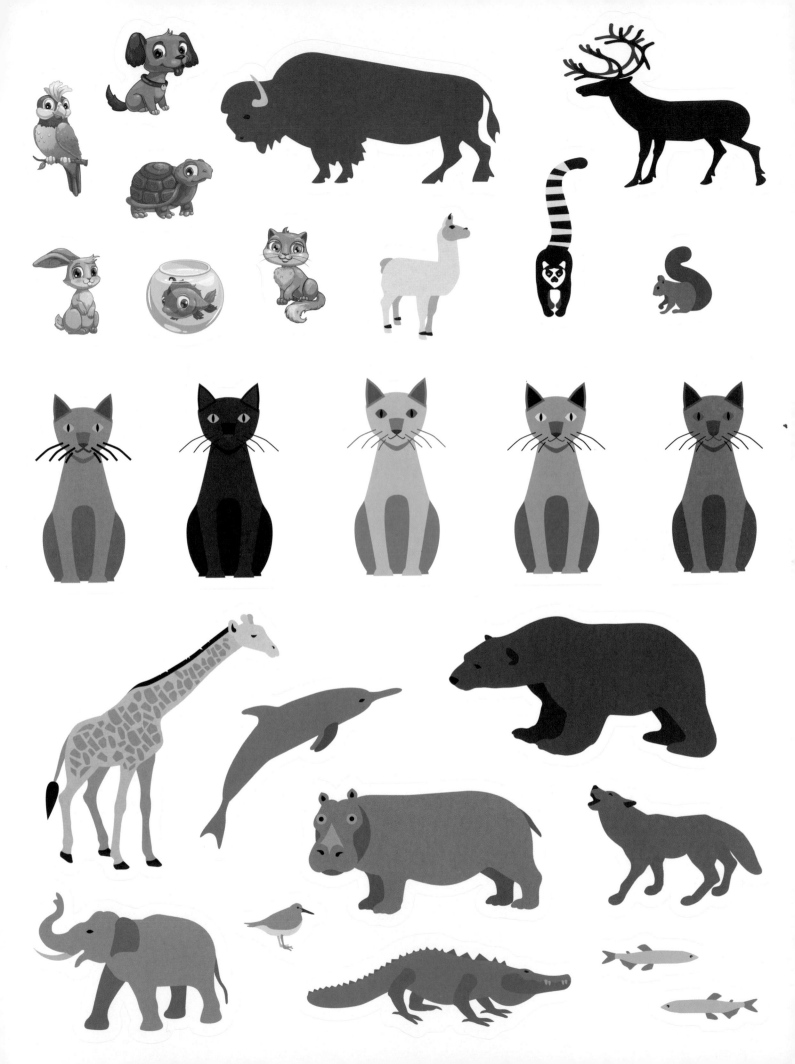

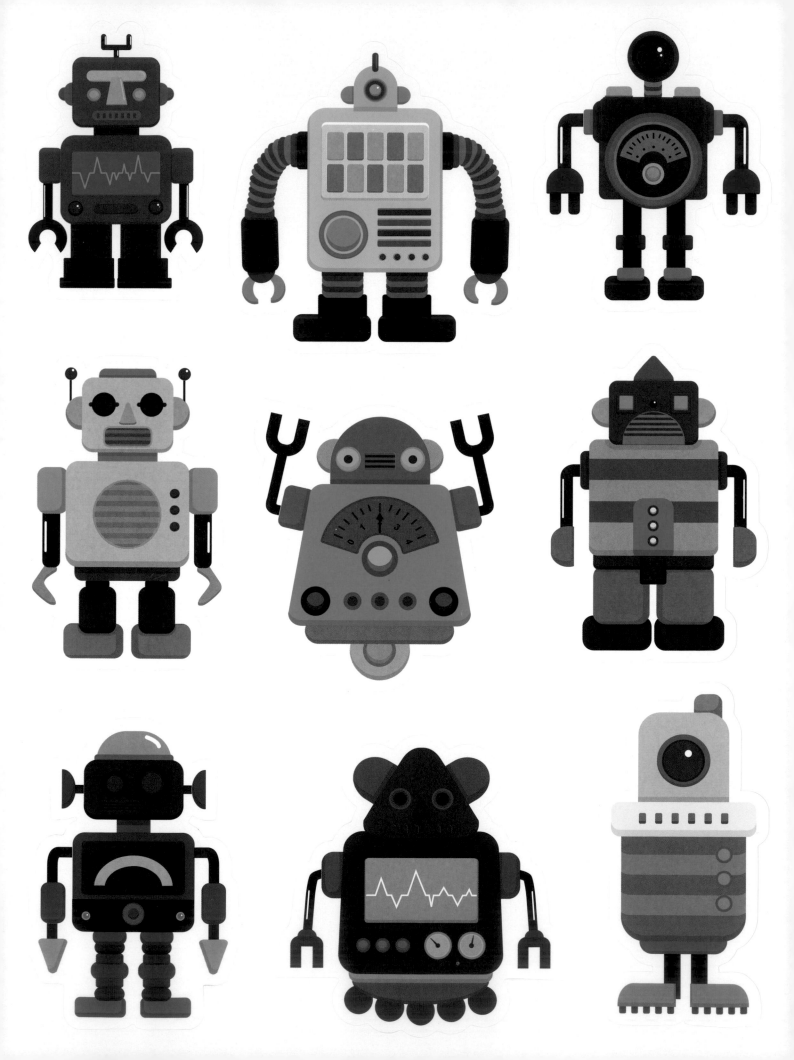